The Jacobites

Cover pictures: Prince Charles Edward Stuart; the Battle of Culloden, 1746.
Inside cover picture:The Two Sisters of Glencoe.
Title page picture: Loch Achtriochtan, Glencoe.
First published in 1995 by Wayland (Publishers) Ltd, 61 Western Road, Hove, East Sussex BN3 1JD, England.

British Library Cataloguing in Publication Data
Rose, Iain
Jacobites
I. Title II. Hook, Richard III. Bull, Peter
941.107

ISBN 0 7502 1516 X

Consultant: Donald Gunn, Education Officer for BBC Scotland.
Editor: Joanna Bentley
Concept design: Derek Lee
Book design and typesetting: Steve Wheele
Printed and bound by B.P.C. Paulton Books, Great Britain

Picture acknowledgements

The publishers wish to thank the following for providing the illustrations in this book: From His Grace the Duke of Atholl's Collection at Blair Castle 8 (left); Bridgeman Art Library cover (both), 29, 30; Copyright British Museum 36; Mary Evans Picture Library 18 (bottom, both), 32 (bottom); Hulton-Deutsch Collection 16, 32 (top); National Trust for Scotland 22; The Royal Collection © Her Majesty the Queen 34; The Royal Commission on the Ancient and Historical Monuments of Scotland 28; Scotland in Focus 15, 23 (A G Firth); Scottish National Portrait Gallery 12 (bottom) 18 (top), 23 (top), 25 (both), 37, 38, 39 (both), 41 (left); Still Moving Picture Company title page (Angus Johnston), 12 (top, Angus Johnston), 14, 21, 24 (bottom, Paul Tomkins), 27; Tony Stone Worldwide 8 (right, Hugh Graham); Ronald Weir 13; West Highland Museum, Fort William 40 (R Matassa), 41 (left); David Whitaker 24 (top).
Artwork by: Peter Bull 6, 9, 13, 14, 17, 19, 20, 21, 30, 33, 35, 38; Richard Hook 7, 10, 11, 26, 31; John Yates cover.

Contents

The Reign of King James

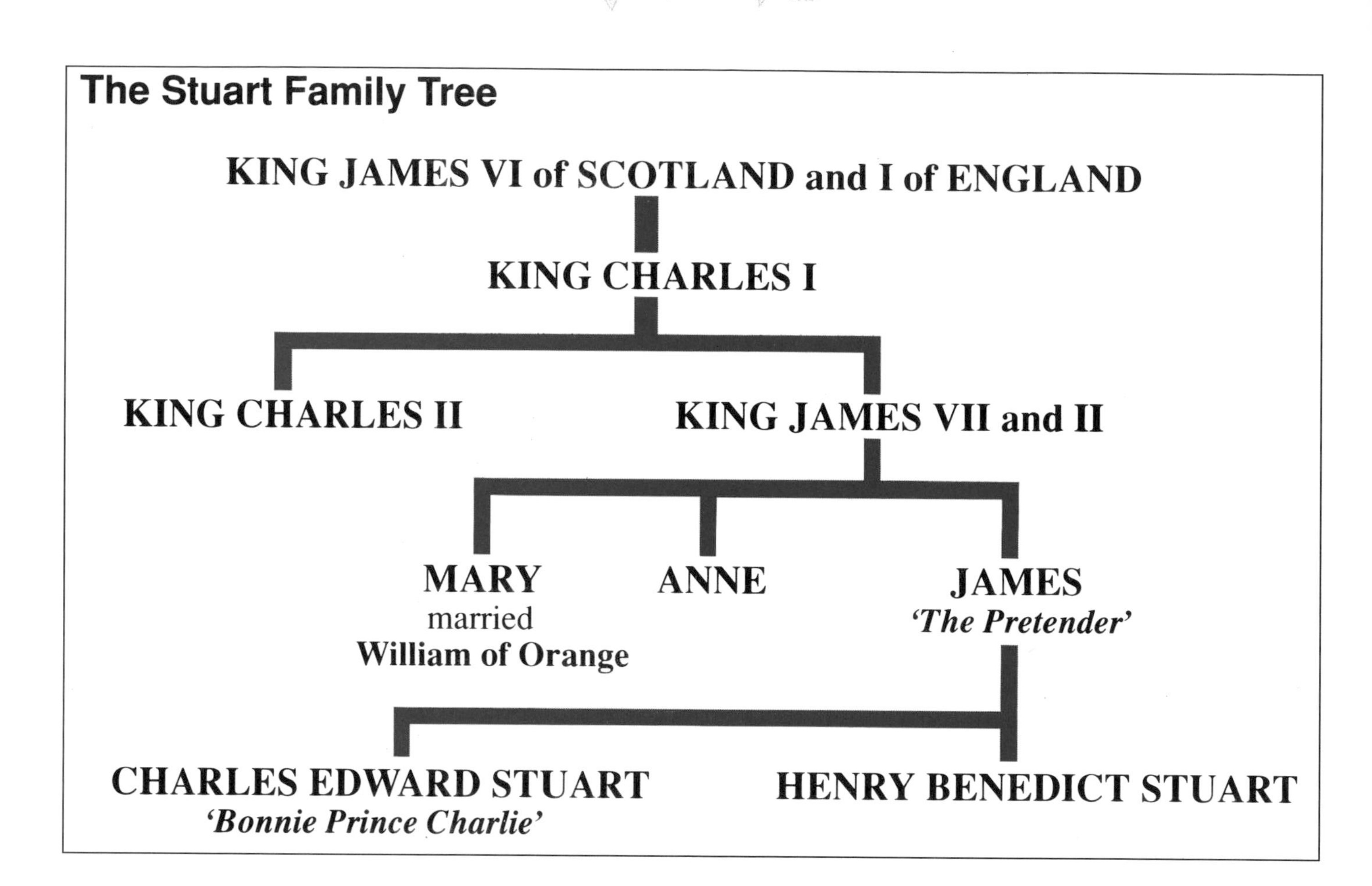

James VII of Scotland and II of England became King in 1685. He ruled two countries because his grandfather, the King of Scotland, had become King of England after Queen Elizabeth I died in 1603. The two countries still kept their own governments and Parliaments.

King James had a short and unhappy reign. The Scots and English Parliaments did not like him wanting lots of power for himself. Also, many people were worried about having a Roman Catholic king ruling countries that were Protestant.

However, James was an old man and people did not think he would live for very long. They thought that, after he died, his daughter, Mary, and her husband, William of Orange, would make far better rulers. They were prepared to wait.

People also knew that William and Mary did not have any children to become rulers after them, but that did not matter because Mary's younger sister, Anne, would become Queen after them and she had many children to become heirs to the throne.

King James had other ideas. He remarried and in June 1688 his son, James was born. Most people were horrified because this boy would become their next king and they thought he would be just as bad as his father. They began to talk of a revolution to get rid of King James and his baby son.

Mary and her husband lived in Holland but they knew what people in Scotland and England were thinking. They decided to act quickly. In November 1688 William of Orange landed at Torbay, England and announced that he and his wife, Mary, were the new King and Queen. Most important people supported them, so King James decided to flee to France. He hoped that the King of France would help him to win back his kingdoms.

King James had a few supporters in France. They called themselves 'Jacobites' because the Latin for James is *'Jacobus'*.

After King James died in 1701, the Jacobites supported his son, whom they called King James VIII and III. However, most people in Scotland and England just nicknamed him 'The Pretender'. This name comes from the French word *'pretendre'* which means 'to claim'. James claimed to be the King of Scotland and England. His son, Prince Charles Edward Stuart, became known as 'the Young Pretender' but he is better known as 'Bonnie Prince Charlie'.

The flight of King James.

Jacobite Clans

The Jacobites hoped that the Highland clans of Scotland would join them and fight for the return of King James.

The clan chiefs were very important in deciding what their clan would do. The chief was the leader of his clan, which was made up of people who believed they were nearly all related and who lived on the clan lands.

These chiefs had a lot of power. They would protect their clansmen in dangerous times and punish them if they broke the law. Chiefs could also give their clansmen orders to fight.

A Highland chief with his weapons.

Highland regiments still have pipe bands.

The clans were very proud of their fighting tradition. Clan pipers composed and played tunes to inspire warriors to fight. Clan bards would make up and recite poems about brave chiefs and great battles from the past.

These tunes and poems were never written down. Older men taught them to young ones and in this way knowledge of music, poetry and clan feuds was passed down for hundreds of years.

Chiefs boasted about the number of fighting men they could command. This was as important to them as the amount of money or land they had.

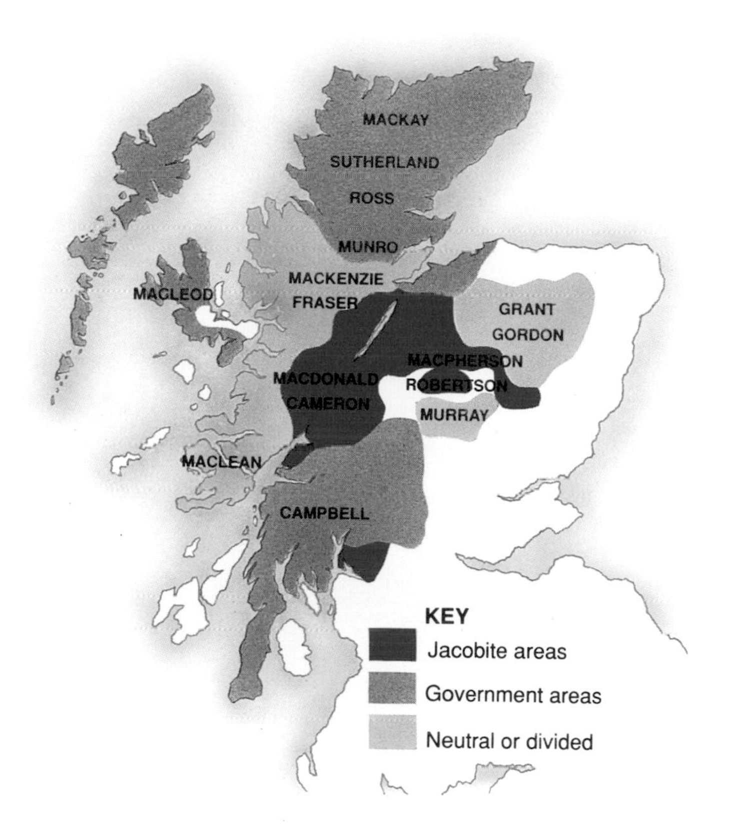

This map shows the clans of the Highlands, and which cause they were loyal to.

The Gaelic Poet Iain Lom lived in Lochaber at this time. In one of his songs he wrote,

Chan e Uilleam tha mì cho déidheil air;
Ach Righ Seumas's a shìol
A dh'òrdaich Dia dhuinn g'ar dìon:
Cha rìgh iasaid d'am fiach dhuinn géilleachdainn.

I don't fancy King William's chances,
But those of King James and his family.
God gave us him to protect us:
We should not obey a 'borrowed' King.

(The Battle of Killiecrankie)
(Cath Raon Ruairidh)

The Jacobite leaders hoped that the chiefs would use their men to fight for King James.

In fact the clans were divided. Some supported William and Mary. Others wanted to keep out of any war. But the rest were willing to fight for King James.

These Jacobite chiefs did not think that a country could change its king in the same way as people could change their clothes. They thought that God had decided who their king should be and that people ought to accept him. They also thought that Queen Mary was a wicked woman for turning against her father, stealing his crown and chasing him out of the country.

Besides, many of them, for example the MacDonalds and Camerons from Lochaber, had supported King Charles I when he fought against Parliament during the Civil War (1642-9). They felt they had been well treated by King James and so they were quite prepared to fight for him and his son.

Clansmen and Redcoats

Highland warriors looked impressive. They carried many different weapons and they wore tartan plaids.

Their plaids were just like big blankets. Indeed, at night time they rolled themselves up in them and went to sleep. During the day, they wrapped themselves in their plaids, which were kept in place by a belt and brooch.

Before they went into battle clansmen quite often took off their plaids and fought in just their vests!

Highlanders were most famous for 'The Highland Charge', which always won the battle for them. Suddenly, they would all run towards the enemy shouting their frightening 'slogans' (*sluagh ghairm* is Gaelic for war cries).

Then, when they were really close, they would fire their muskets all at once. After that they would carry on racing towards their enemies and use their huge swords to cut them to pieces.

They carried targes (shields) to protect themselves. The targe often had a big pointed spike in the middle, which made it another dangerous weapon.

For hand-to-hand fighting they also had a dirk (a big knife). Some men even carried pistols.

Right: A Highland warrior.
Opposite: A Redcoat.

Soldiers in King William's army wore red coats as part of their uniform. They were often called 'redcoats'. The Highlanders called them '*Saighdearan dearg*' (red soldiers).

Redcoats were full-time soldiers who had spent years being trained how to fight. This training emphasized discipline and drill. Every man had to learn to do exactly the same as all the others, especially when they had to march in step. You can still see this kind of marching in ceremonies like 'Trooping the Colour'.

Soldiers had to be drilled in how to use their muskets, because loading and firing a musket was a difficult and complicated thing to do.

Before any battle the soldiers had to prepare cartridges in which a musket ball and gunpowder were wrapped together in special paper.

During the battle a soldier had to push one of these cartridges down the barrel of his musket, using a ramrod. He had to remember to remove the ramrod because, if he forgot, he would fire it at the enemy and be unable to load his musket again!

After that, he had to fill the firing pan of his musket with gunpowder and aim at the enemy. Only then could he pull the trigger.

When the trigger hit the side of the firing pan a small piece of flint caused a spark, which set fire to the gunpowder there. That fire made the cartridge in the musket explode, so that the musket ball was fired towards the enemy.

For hand-to-hand fighting the redcoats used bayonets. These were long knives clipped to the end of their muskets. Their officers used swords.

The first Jacobite Rising

The Pass of Killiecrankie.

At first the Scottish Jacobites were very slow to get organized. They did not realise how unpopular James VII and II was.

John Graham of Claverhouse tried to organize an army in the south and east of Scotland but hardly anybody joined him. Many Scots disliked him and called him 'Bluidy Clavers' (Bloody Claverhouse) because of the way he had murdered Protestants who did not like the religious rule of James VII and II.

On the other hand, the Jacobites called him 'Bonnie Dundee' and joined the Highland army he gathered in Lochaber.

John Graham of Claverhouse.

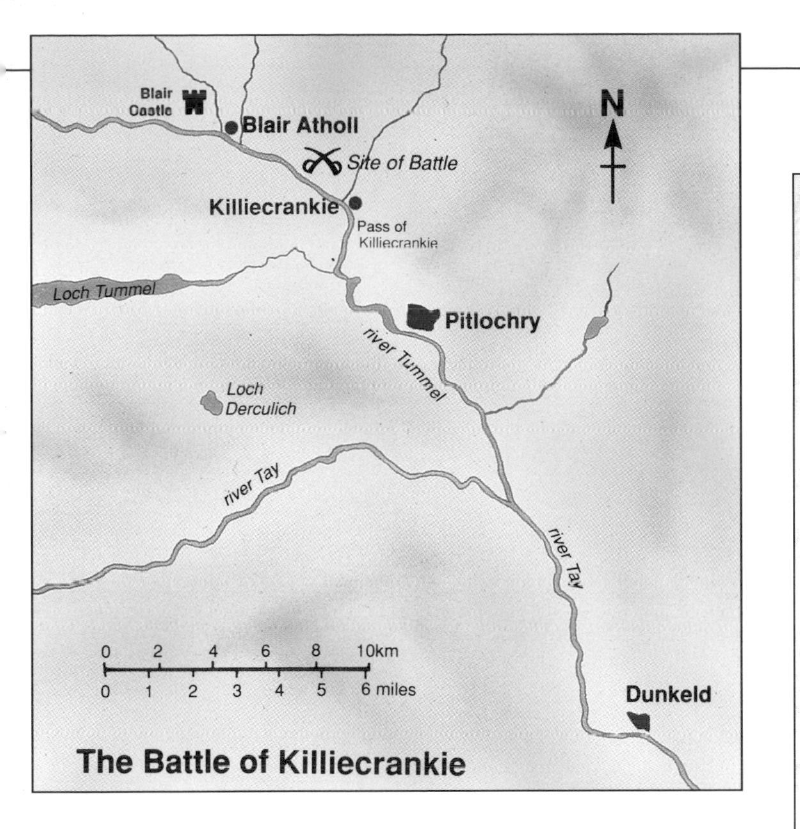

Claverhouse led his army southwards towards the Lowlands of Scotland. At the same time General MacKay led King William's army northwards. The two armies met in the narrow Pass of Killiecrankie between Blair Atholl and Pitlochry.

The Highlanders took cover on the bushy hillside and watched MacKay's men for two hours before they launched their terrific charge. This sudden, ferocious attack was too much for MacKay's redcoats. They turned and fled, leaving many dead and wounded men behind them.

The Jacobites had won the battle, but a lot of their men had been killed during their charge.

Claverhouse was also killed and without his leadership the Jacobite army lost heart. Their advance was stopped at Dunkeld and many men simply went home.

THE LEGEND OF BONNIE DUNDEE.

Many people hated John Graham of Claverhouse so much that they believed he had been sent by the Devil. They thought that the Devil was protecting him and that he could be killed only by a silver bullet. During the Battle of Killiecrankie a wounded soldier tore a silver button from his tunic and fired it at 'Bluidy Clavers'.
The bullet went through his breastplate and wounded him very seriously in the chest. He had to be carried away from the battlefield and died soon after he found out that his army had won the battle.

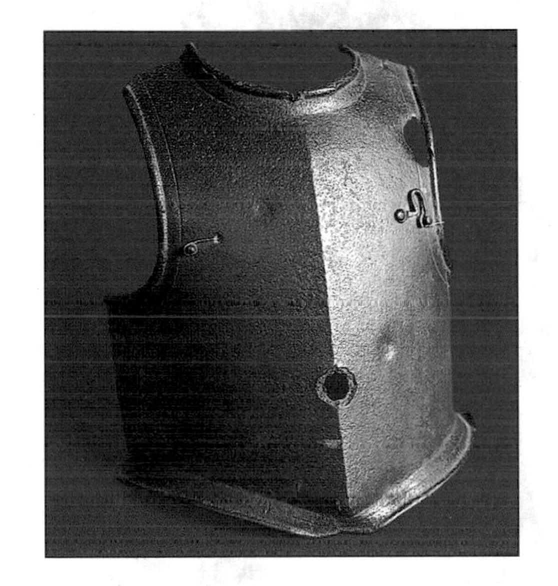

Claverhouse's breastplate showing the hole made by the bullet that killed him.

The Massacre of Glencoe

The valley of Glencoe.

King William wanted to make sure that the Jacobite chiefs would obey him, so he sent his soldiers into the Highlands to keep an eye on them. These soldiers built Fort William right in the middle of Lochaber.

Then King William told the Jacobite chiefs that they had to make a promise to obey him. He gave them until 30 December 1691 to make their promises or else they would be punished.

MacIain, the old chief of the MacDonalds of Glencoe, waited until the very last day before he went to make his promise at Fort William. When he got there he was told he could only make his promise in front of the Sheriff of Argyll at Inveraray.

It took the old man five days to walk there through blizzards and very deep snow. When he reached Inveraray MacIain explained why he was late and then he made his promise to obey King

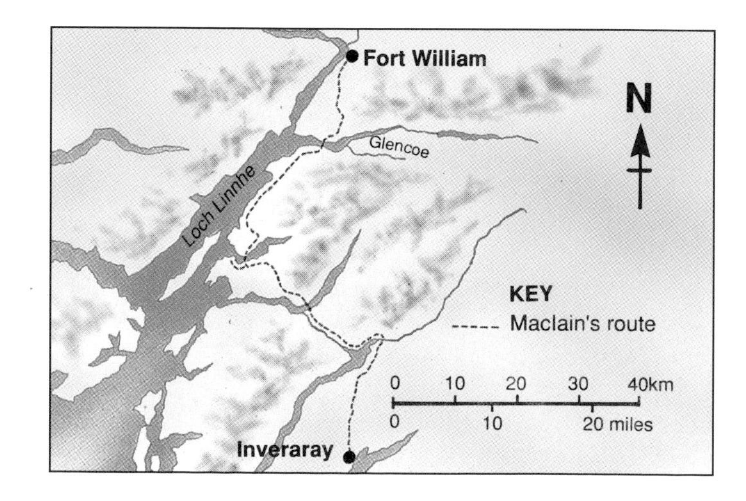

William. After that he thought everything would be fine.

He was wrong.

King William's government decided to make an example of the MacDonalds by killing the whole clan. They made very careful plans. They sent so many soldiers to Fort William that it did not have room for all of them. Local people had to give these extra soldiers beds.

The MacDonalds of Glencoe were not surprised when some soldiers came to stay with them. They did not know that these soldiers would be used to kill them. Indeed, nobody knew about the plans until the very last minute.

The government gave the soldiers in Glencoe orders to murder the families they were staying with at five o'clock in the morning of 13 February 1692. They thought the MacDonalds would be in their beds so it would be easy to kill them all. Extra soldiers from Fort William were sent to block the roads out of Glencoe to make sure that nobody could escape.

Their plan did not work. A terrible blizzard stopped the soldiers from Fort William reaching Glencoe in time. The soldiers in Glencoe got lost in the snow, so many MacDonalds escaped and hid in the mountains.

Some soldiers may even have helped the people to escape because they thought it was wrong to kill people in this way. But others killed as many MacDonalds as they could. 38 people were killed but about 450 escaped.

The MacDonalds' monument at Glencoe.

Maclain was asleep when the soldiers came to his house.

When he heard them he thought that they were calling to say 'Goodbye' before they left Glencoe. He jumped out of his bed and ordered his servants to give them a farewell drink.

He was getting dressed when he was shot dead. His wife was robbed and left to lie in the snow. She died from the cold.

The Act of Union

When William and Mary died, Mary's sister, Anne, became Queen in 1702. Unfortunately, all of her children had died, so there was a problem about who would rule after her.

The English Parliament decided that their next ruler would have to be a Protestant member of the British Royal Family. That was why they chose Anne's second cousin, Sophia, who was married to a German prince, the Elector of Hanover.

The Scottish Parliament decided that it did not want to have the same ruler as England any more. It tried to find another Protestant member of the Stuart Royal Family.

Queen Anne receiving the Treaty of Union in 1707.

The English Parliament was very upset about this because in the past there had been many wars between England and Scotland. The French and Scots had often helped each other to fight the English. It was worried about more wars like this happening in the future. So the English Parliament decided it wanted the Scottish Parliament to join it, to make a new country called the United Kingdom of Great Britain.

This suggestion was not popular in Scotland, but the English Parliament threatened to make war on the Scots if they did not agree. It also paid huge amounts of money to the Scottish Members of Parliament to make sure that they voted for the Act of Union.

The St. Andrew's Cross of Scotland and the St.George's Cross of England were put together to produce a new flag. The modern Union flag was created when the Irish St. Patrick's Cross was added when Ireland joined the Union in 1800.

There were riots in Scotland when its Parliament agreed to the Act of Union of 1707.

Jacobites stirred up trouble about the Act of Union. They hoped to win extra support in Scotland, especially after the Scots were made to pay new taxes!

When the King of France saw what was happening in Scotland, he decided to help a Jacobite rising there. Great Britain and France were at war and he saw a chance to spread this war to Scotland.

King James VII and II had died in 1701. After that his son called himself King James VIII and III. (In Scotland and England he was usually called 'The Pretender'). He wanted to claim back the kingdoms he had left as a baby in 1688.

In 1708 James got his chance. Just a year after the unpopular Act of Union the King of France gave him ships and 5,000 soldiers to help him to win back his kingdom.

Unfortunately, the French plan did not work. King James became very ill with measles and could not join the attack. The British Royal Navy spotted the French ships while they were still at sea and the French commander decided the attack was too dangerous. So he took everyone back to France!

Seven years later Queen Anne died. Sophia had also died, so the next British ruler was her son, George, Elector of Hanover.

Hardly anyone was happy about being ruled by *'a wee bit German Lairdie'*, who did not even speak English! The Jacobites caused as much trouble as they could. They hoped that the people would prefer King James VIII and III. They planned another uprising.

The '15

John, Earl of Mar, wanted a good job from the new King George I. However, other men who wanted to work for King George told him that Mar was a secret Jacobite. So, when Mar went to see George I, the King ignored him. Mar was furious! The very next day he sailed to Scotland to start a Jacobite rising.

Unfortunately, Mar was not a very good general. It took him a long time to gather an army and when he got one he did not know what to do with it. He had hoped for help from France, but the French king died and the French sent no help at all.

Mar's supporters also made silly mistakes. They planned to capture Edinburgh Castle by climbing up rope ladders and surprising its garrison. But their ladders were too short and, while they were waiting for more rope, the garrison caught them!

John, Earl of Mar, led the '15.

King George's supporters were more organized. Although his army was much smaller than Mar's, their leader, the Duke of Argyll, managed to capture Stirling Castle. This castle was very important because it controlled the main route from the north to the south of Scotland. Mar's army was trapped in the north.

Both Stirling Castle (left) and Edinburgh Castle (right) are on top of very steep hills. They control the countryside for miles around.

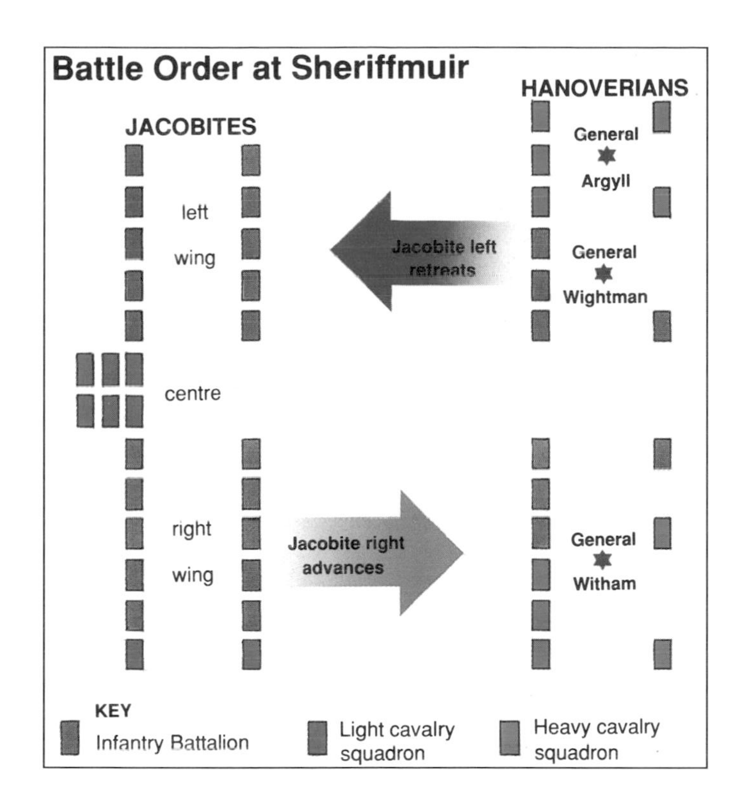

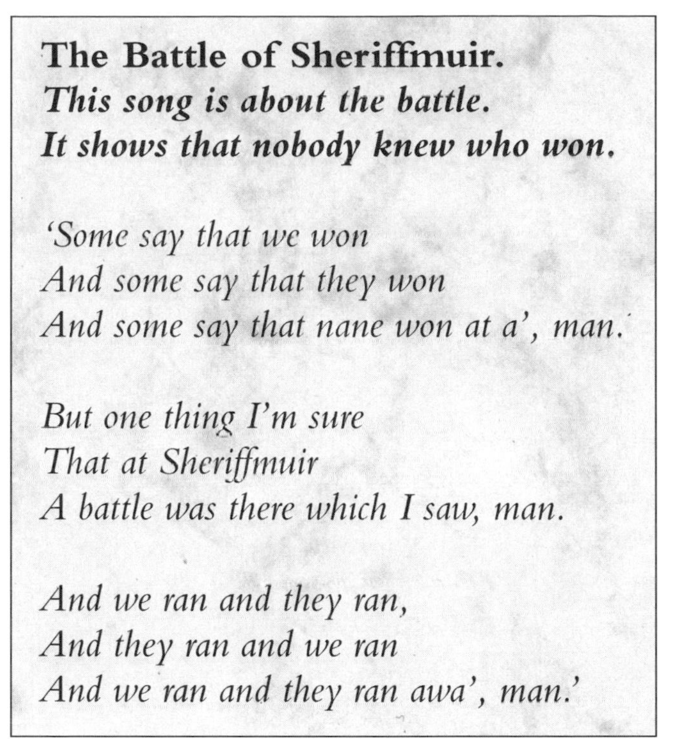

The Battle of Sheriffmuir.
This song is about the battle.
It shows that nobody knew who won.

'Some say that we won
And some say that they won
And some say that nane won at a', man.

But one thing I'm sure
That at Sheriffmuir
A battle was there which I saw, man.

And we ran and they ran,
And they ran and we ran
And we ran and they ran awa', man.'

Finally, Mar marched to attack Stirling. Argyll's army advanced to stop him before he reached the town and a battle was fought at Sheriffmuir, just beside Dunblane.

The Battle of Sheriffmuir did not produce a clear result. Mar's army was divided into three groups - the left wing, the centre and the right wing. The right wing beat the soldiers they faced, but the left wing was defeated. After that the fighting stopped and both armies went back to their camps for the night.

On the day of the Battle of Sheriffmuir the Jacobites got the news that a small Jacobite army in England had been beaten at Preston. They were disappointed by that. They were also short of money and short of food. So they gave up and went home.

Six weeks later James, the 'Old Pretender', finally arrived at Peterhead in Scotland. He did not have any extra French help for the Jacobites and, although he was crowned King, nobody paid much attention to him. After a few weeks he went back to France.

The Jacobites did not give up. In 1719, they got Spanish help for another rising. However, a Government ship blew up Eilean Donan Castle, where they had stored their supplies. Then a Government army defeated the Spaniards at Bealach nan Spainteach (The Pass of the Spaniards), not far from Eilean Donan Castle.

Another Jacobite rising had been defeated, but the Government of King George I decided to do something to control the Highlands.

Controlling the Highlands

King George's Government planned to stop any further trouble in the Highlands. They told the Highlanders to give them all their weapons. The Highlanders simply hid their good weapons and gave them their old, broken ones that were no good!

The Government recruited Highland soldiers who supported King George to keep an eye on the Jacobites. These soldiers became known as 'The Black Watch' *(Am Freiceadan Dubh)* because they wore a dark tartan and looked very different from ordinary soldiers, the 'redcoats' *(saighdearan dearg)*.

Then the Government built more forts and barracks in the Highlands for its soldiers. It built forts at Inverness and Cille Chumein (Fort Augustus), and made Fort William bigger. Barracks were built at Ruthven, Bernera and Inversnaid.

New roads made it easier for soldiers to march between these forts and for the Government to send more men to the Highlands if the Jacobites started another rising.

General Wade's roads allowed the redcoats to march between the forts in the Highlands.

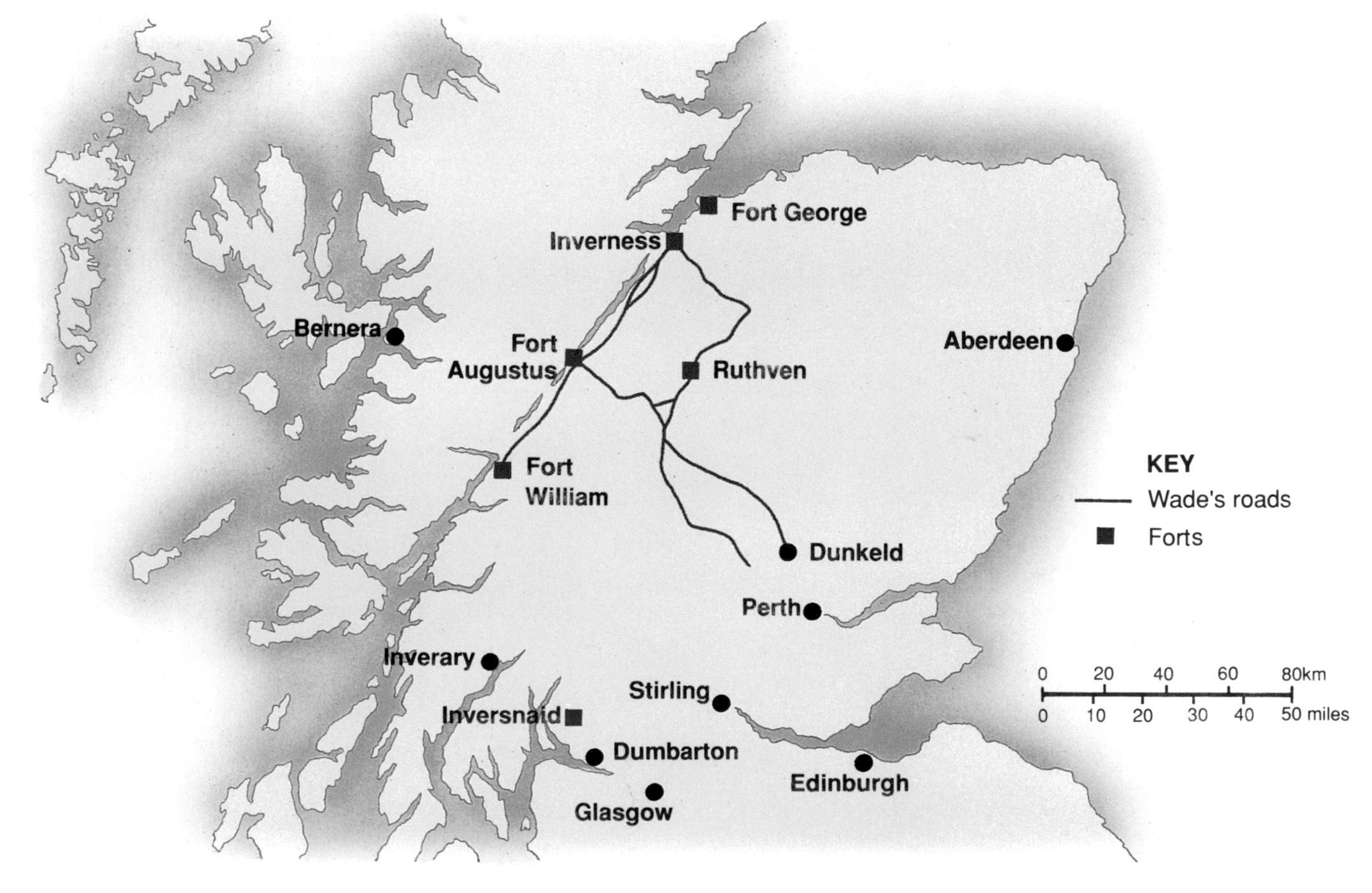

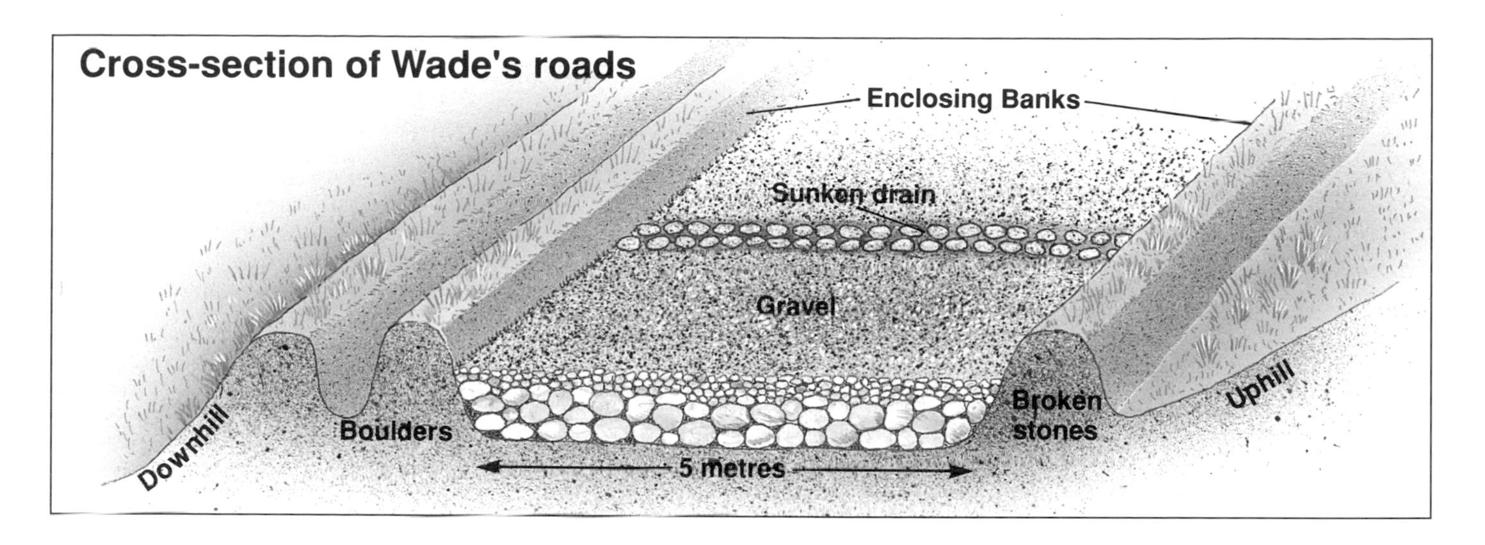

General Wade was put in charge of building these roads and forts. When he began there were no proper roads or bridges in the Highlands.

His soldiers built 416 km (260 miles) of 'military roads' using methods like the ones the Romans had used. Their roads were very straight and had a solid stone base with broken stones and gravel on top. They also built bridges across the deep rivers that cut across Scotland.

After General Wade's first building programme, another 1330 km (830 miles) of military roads and even more bridges were built. The Government was spending a lot of money to make sure it controlled the Highlands.

But all the time the Jacobites were waiting for a chance to try again. These fine new roads would make it easier for them to move about as well !

General Wade's bridge at Aberfeldy. He built more than forty other bridges.

The Rash Adventure

HMS *Lion* in battle with the *Elizabeth*. The *du Teillay* escaped to take Prince Charles to Scotland.

In 1744 Britain was ruled by King George II, the son of George I. That year, Britain and France went to war again. The Jacobites hoped that this time the French would send them enough help to start a successful rising.

The Pretender's son, Charles Edward Stuart, who is often called 'Bonnie Prince Charlie', left Rome, where he was staying with his father, and went to Paris.

He was in luck. King Louis XV of France was gathering men, weapons and supplies for him. The French planned to land this new Jacobite army in England.

Just when everything was ready, a great storm wrecked the French fleet. Most of the supplies were lost and the King of France gave up the idea of helping Prince Charles.

Charles was very disappointed, but he did not give up. He sold some things and then borrowed enough money to buy 1,500 muskets, 1,800 broadswords and some small cannon.

He also hired two French ships, the *Elizabeth* and the *du Teillay*, to carry him and his weapons to Scotland. Prince Charles was going to start a rising all by himself!

Charles Edward Stuart. This was drawn when Prince Charles was in Edinburgh.

Just after his ships left harbour, a British warship, the *Lion*, attacked the Prince's ships. The *Elizabeth* was so badly damaged that it had to go back to France. Unfortunately, it had all his weapons on board .

On board the *du Teillay* Prince Charles continued his journey to Scotland. He had seven friends with him. That was all the support he brought for the Scottish Jacobites.

He arrived first at the little island of Eriskay, in the Outer Hebrides. When the chief there discovered that the Prince had no French help, he told him to go home. The Prince replied, 'I have come home, sir' and tried to persuade him to support this latest Jacobite rising.

The *du Teillay* then sailed to Loch nan Uamh in Lochaber. There the ship dropped anchor and Prince Charles went ashore to start his 'Rash Adventure'. It is usually known as 'The '45'.

This group of trees represents the Seven Men of Moidart, who were Prince Charles's loyal supporters on his arrival in Scotland. Only five of the trees remain.

Persuading the Chiefs

At first Prince Charles did not want the Government of George II to know that he was in Scotland. Secretly, he invited all the Jacobite chiefs in Lochaber to meet him to make their plans.

Most of the MacDonald chiefs told him to go home. They were worried because he had brought no men or weapons with him. However, the Prince was able to persuade them to join him. He said that French help would arrive and that he would also get help from Jacobites in England.

Below: Loch nan Uamh. Prince Charles arrived at this lonely loch to start his rebellion in 1745 and left from it after his rising failed in 1746.

When the Prince's messenger arrived at Achnacarry, Lochiel, the chief of the Camerons, was busy planting trees beside his house. Lochiel's younger brother warned him not even to see the Prince, 'because,' he said 'if you set eyes on him he will persuade you.'

Below: Lochiel's trees are still growing at Achnacarry.

Duncan Forbes persuaded many chiefs not to join Prince Charles.

Lochiel decided to visit the Prince to tell him to go back to France. Prince Charles promised him French men, money and weapons to support the rising and finally he tried to shame Lochiel into joining him. The Prince said:

> 'In a few days I will announce that I have come to Britain to win my crown or to die. Lochiel, whom my father often said was our best supporter, can stay at home and read about my fate in the newspapers.'

Lochiel then promised to join the Prince and to bring him eight hundred men.

Without Lochiel's support Prince Charles would not have had enough men for an army and there would have been no rising in 1745. Lochiel's decision persuaded other chiefs to send their men as well. Prince Charles's army grew.

The Government was not surprised that Prince Charles was in Scotland. However, they were astonished that he had brought no support with him. Without French help they thought he had no chance of success.

Duncan Forbes of Culloden, a Government supporter who lived just outside Inverness, had been very busy persuading the Highland chiefs in that area not to support Prince Charles. He warned them of the dangers of getting mixed up in another rising, which he was certain would end in disaster for the Jacobites.

Most of these chiefs listened to his warnings. Very few of them joined Prince Charles during the '45. Some joined the Government army, which the Jacobites called 'Hanoverian' because they supported the King George who came from Hanover.

But, in Lochaber, the Jacobite clans were gathering.

Glenfinnan

The Raising of the Standard at Glenfinnan 19th August, 1745.

Prince Charles had arranged to meet the Jacobite chiefs with their soldiers at Glenfinnan on 19 August, 1745.

There was a lot of excitement about the rising. Already, a group of eighty Hanoverian soldiers had been ambushed near Fort William and forced to surrender to the Jacobites. They were very embarrassed to discover that they had been tricked by only a dozen clansmen. The Jacobites thought this early victory was a good sign.

The ladies of the area had been very busy making a big red, white and blue flag for Prince Charles's army.

But when he arrived at Glenfinnan there was hardly anybody there. Lochiel was late. He did not arrive with his eight hundred clansmen until later in the afternoon. Prince Charles joined four or five hundred MacDonalds who had already arrived.

Then, at about five o'clock, the ceremony called 'The Raising of the Standard' began. The very old Marquis of Tullibardine, who had fought in the risings of 1715 and 1719, unrolled Prince Charles's flag and announced that James VIII and III was King.

There was a lot of cheering and people shouted 'Long live King James VIII and Prince Charles, prosperity to Scotland, and no Union!' This tells us why many people supported the '45.

But there were other reasons as well. Some men wanted an excuse to get even with old enemies. They hoped that joining in this rising would give them a chance to do so.

Others joined in for the money. The Earl of Kilmarnock said, 'I didn't care a farthing for the two Kings (James or George II), but I was starving and I must eat.'

Other clansmen were there because their chiefs had made them come. Lochiel's men had been warned that, 'if they did not come he would instantly burn all their houses and cripple their cattle.' Another chief said, 'They must go or be destroyed'.

As far as George II was concerned, every man who joined Prince Charles was a rebel and deserved to be killed. Life could be very hard on ordinary people.

The tower and monument at Glenfinnan were built many years after the rising. The statue should have been of Prince Charles but the sculptor made a mistake. He copied a painting of a young man who was killed fighting for Prince Charles. The statue now stands for all the men who were killed while fighting for the Jacobites.

Capturing Edinburgh

Two days later, the Jacobite army left Glenfinnan and began its march to London. It stopped at Fassifern, which was the home of Lochiel's brother. He had tried to stop Lochiel joining in the rising and he quite deliberately left home that day to show that he did not support Prince Charles.

Some clansmen took little white roses from his garden as badges for their bonnets. After that, the white rose became a Jacobite sign. It was called 'The White Cockade'.

General Wade's new roads allowed the Jacobites to move quickly through the Highlands. In fact, they moved so quickly that they got past General Cope, who was moving his troops north to meet them.

There was nobody to stop the Jacobites reaching Edinburgh, the capital city of Scotland. But the Town Council of Edinburgh locked the city gates against them. They were frightened of the Jacobites, especially with an army of what they thought would be 'wild' Highlanders!

The Jacobites tricked their way into the city. When the Town Council sent messengers to the Jacobites, Lochiel secretly followed them back to the city. When the city gates were opened to let the messengers in, Lochiel's men charged, captured the gate and let in the rest of the Jacobite army.

Prince Charles had captured the capital city of Scotland. His good looks and charm soon won over the ladies of Edinburgh. They did think 'Charlie is my Darling', which later became a Jacobite song.

In 1745 Edinburgh still had a wall around it with gates that were shut at night.

The Jacobite Rose. It became a Jacobite badge and was used to decorate glasses and other objects. In this design the flower stands for King James VIII and two rosebuds represent his sons: Charles Edward Stuart and Henry Benedict Stuart.

Hey, Johnnie Cope

Hey, Johnnie Cope, are ye waukin' yet,
And are yer drums a'beating yet?
If ye were waukin' I would wait,
tae gang tae the coals in the mornin'.

The Jacobites poked fun at General Cope by saying that he was beaten by sleeping in.

The men of Edinburgh were not so sure. They were suspicious of Prince Charles and the kind of ruler he would be. In particular they did not like him being a Catholic.

They knew that Edinburgh Castle had not been captured, and that General Cope was bringing his army to Edinburgh. They put up with Charles, but hoped that he would be defeated quickly.

When Cope got close to Edinburgh the Jacobite army set off to fight him. Cope had 2,500 soldiers and had chosen a good place to fight at Prestonpans. The Jacobite army was about the same size but its General, Lord George Murray, thought it was too dangerous to march straight up to attack Cope. Instead, he decided to surprise Cope by marching during the night to attack him from a quite different direction, which, he thought, suited the Highlanders better.

The plan worked: Cope's army was caught by surprise and defeated. The Jacobites then told everybody they had won because Cope's soldiers were still in their beds!

After the Battle of Prestonpans there was no doubt that Prince Charles controlled Scotland. But he wanted to control England as well, so his army marched southwards.

The Jacobites Advance

King George II sent General Wade with an army to stop the Jacobites. This army expected them to march down the east coast of England, but instead of doing this, the Jacobites went to Carlisle and down the west coast. There were no soldiers there to stop them and their army advanced very quickly.

It took them only five weeks to reach Derby, which was just 203 km (127 miles) from London. People thought that the Jacobites could not be stopped!

In London there was panic. People expected the terrifying Jacobite army to arrive at any minute. On 'Black Friday', the streets of London were deserted while people packed their belongings and got ready to leave the city, or hid their valuables so they could not be stolen.

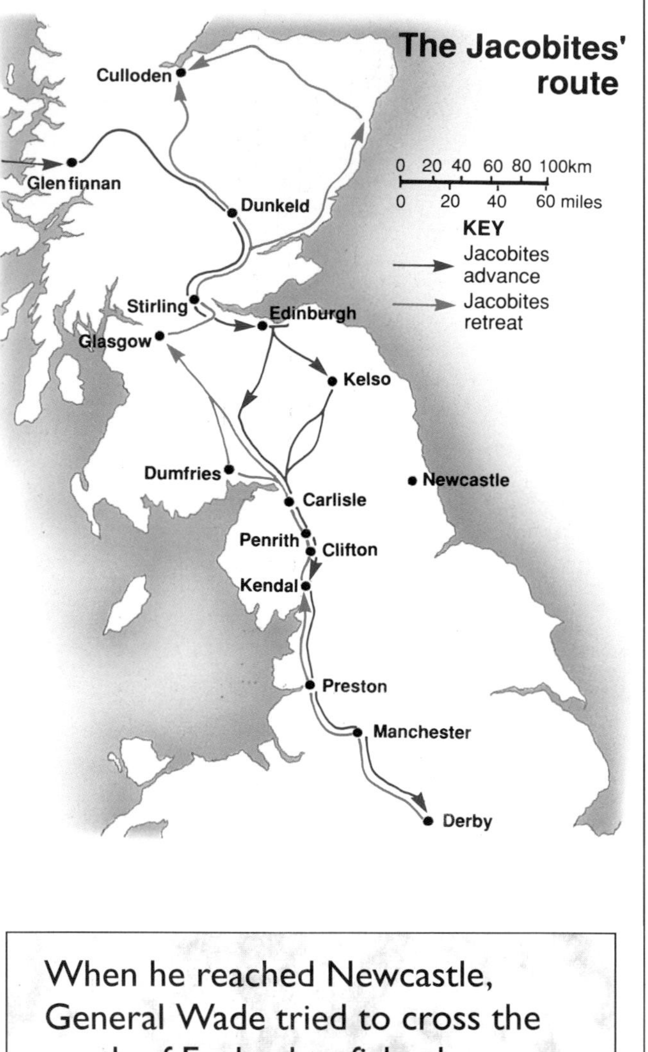

King George II.

When he reached Newcastle, General Wade tried to cross the north of England to fight the Jacobites.
But there were no roads there and the weather was dreadful. His army got stuck!
At the time this poem was written:
'Old Grandmother Wade'
'Whose cunning's so quick, but whose motions so slow
That the rebels marched on while he stuck in the snow!'

There was even a story that King George II had his bags packed and was ready to go back to Hanover!

In Derby, the Jacobite leaders were meeting in a Council of War. The Highland chiefs were very worried. Only 200 Englishmen had joined their army. They did not think they could capture London with an army of only 5,000 men.

Besides, there was no sign of the French help which Prince Charles had promised them. They began to wonder if the French would ever send help. Some chiefs began to doubt if Prince Charles had been telling the truth when he promised them French help. He might have told them lies just to get them to fight for him.

Finally, the chiefs knew that huge numbers of Hanoverian soldiers were gathering all around them in three big armies. They wanted to go back to Scotland to get more men and to give more time for French help to arrive. They did not want to be beaten, a long way from home, in England.

The Council Meeting at Derby. Charles fell out with the chiefs for not going on to London.

Prince Charles was furious. He wanted to go on to London where he thought the people would be delighted to see him. He never understood that most people did not want him as King.

The meeting with the chiefs got very bad tempered. Charles felt they were letting him down at the very last minute. The chiefs were certain that going on to London was far too dangerous.

Finally, Charles agreed to return to Scotland. But he said that he would never take advice from the chiefs again. After that there was always trouble between Charles's Irish friends and the Highland chiefs.

The Jacobite army marched back to Scotland but it was still not beaten.

The Jacobites Retreat

As the Jacobites moved northwards, they were followed by a Hanoverian army led by the Duke of Cumberland, King George's son. He fought them in a small battle at Clifton, but usually he just watched their retreat.

When they left Carlisle, Prince Charles insisted that the Jacobites left soldiers there. He wanted to show that he controlled at least one English town of importance. The Jacobite chiefs warned him that this was silly, but Charles insisted. So 400 men were left to defend Carlisle.

After only two days' fighting Cumberland captured Carlisle. He hanged the Jacobite officers there and sent the other prisoners abroad to be slaves for seven years.

Above: The Duke of Cumberland.

Left: The execution of the Jacobite officers at Carlisle. The soldiers were sent away to be slaves.

The Jacobites reached Glasgow on Boxing Day, 1745. The city was not pleased to see them and nobody cheered them when they arrived.

Prince Charles demanded that the Town Council should give his soldiers new clothes. Otherwise, he threatened he would make an example of them 'to strike terror in other places'. Lochiel persuaded the Prince not to destroy Glasgow and just over a week later the Jacobites left the city.

They wanted to capture Stirling Castle because it controlled all the roads to the north of Scotland. There, a fresh Jacobite army joined them. This gave the Prince an army of about 8,000 men.

He needed them. While he was attacking Stirling Castle a Hanoverian army, under General Hawley, advanced towards Stirling. Lord George Murray led the Jacobites to stop the Hanoverians in a battle which was fought near Falkirk.

Hawley was very confident. He believed that his horsemen could easily defeat the Jacobites.

He was wrong. Lord George Murray told his men to wait until the horses were only ten yards away before they fired. Then, they all fired at once. Eighty horsemen fell dead and the rest all ran away.

After that the Highlanders charged and Hawley's army was defeated. Hawley was so furious that he smashed his sword on the market cross at Falkirk.

The Jacobites went back to attacking Stirling Castle. This was hopeless because they had hardly any cannons and the man in charge of them was useless. Their attack failed. They decided to retreat to the Highlands to gather men and to wait for French help.

Cumberland and his men followed them and both armies prepared for a show-down.

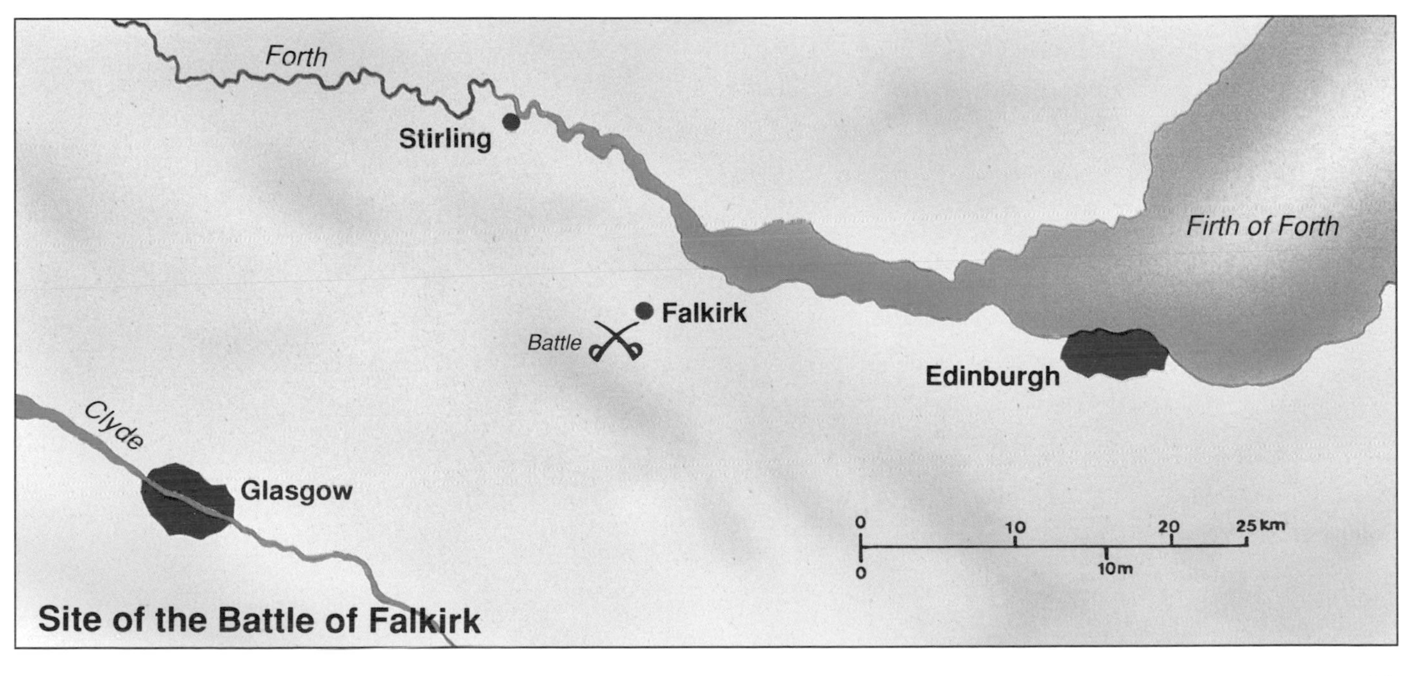

Site of the Battle of Falkirk

Culloden

Morier painted his picture of the Battle of Culloden in 1748. He used Jacobite prisoners to make sure he got the Highlanders looking as they did during the battle.

Prince Charles had problems. He had run out of money. The Royal Navy had stopped a French ship carrying gold for him. Without money his army was short of supplies and the soldiers were hungry because there was no food. Some of them wanted to go home. There were more arguments between the chiefs and the Prince's Irish advisers.

O'Sullivan wanted to fight the Duke of Cumberland at Culloden. The chiefs said that place did not suit their way of fighting. Indeed, they claimed, it suited the Hanoverians.

Lord George Murray then agreed to try and surprise Cumberland by a night attack on his camp at Nairn.

The plan failed. Many Jacobites had gone away to find food and the others were too cold and hungry to march fast enough. Lord George decided it was too dangerous to attack and he led his men back to Culloden. Prince Charles did not understand why the plan had failed and he blamed Lord George.

The cold, tired and hungry Jacobite army then formed up at Culloden. A strong wind was driving sleet right into their faces.

There were more arguments. It was said that the MacDonalds were angry because they had been placed on the left of the army. They wanted to be on the right, where they had always fought since the time of King Robert Bruce. They felt they had been insulted.

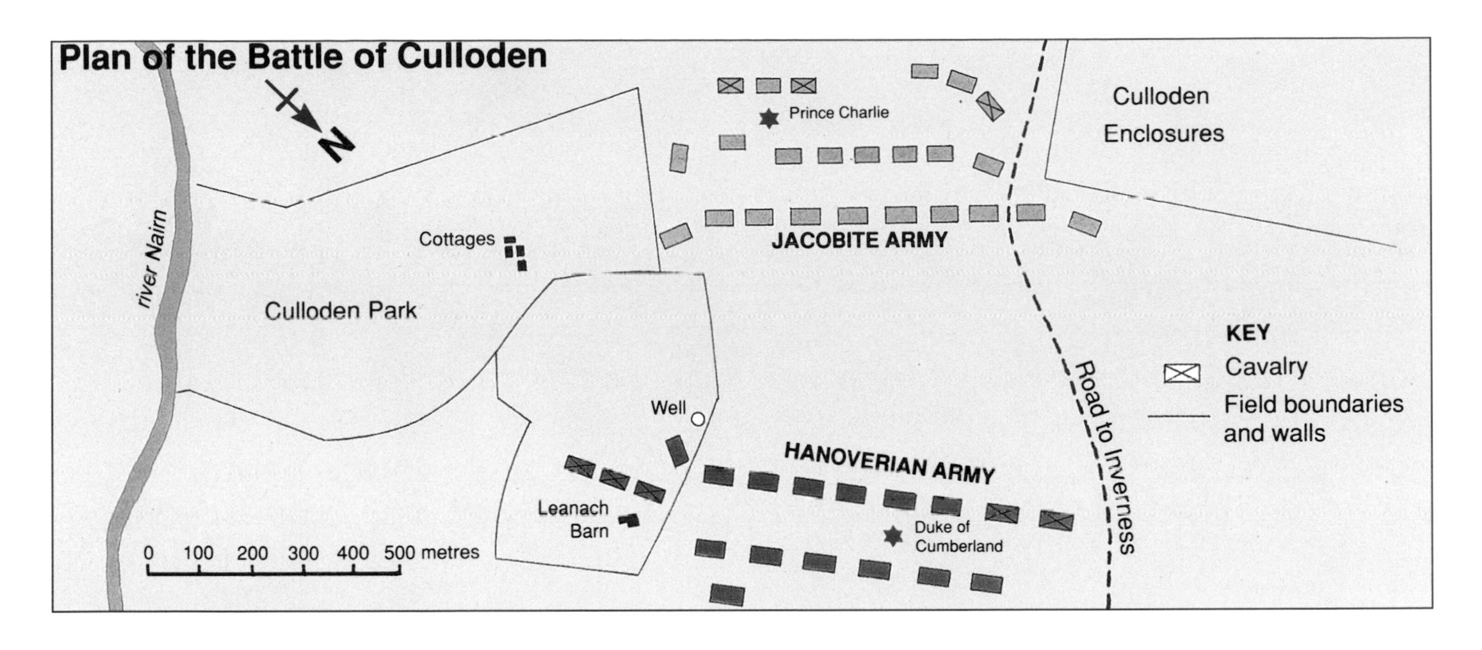

While the 5,000 Jacobites were lining up, Cumberland's men arrived. He had 9,000 soldiers. There were redcoats, cavalry and Highland clansmen, who made up one third of the Hanoverian army. Unlike the Jacobites, these men were well fed, armed and had slept.

The battle began just after one o'clock, when the Jacobites began to fire cannon at the Hanoverians. They had only a few guns and they did very little damage. The Hanoverians had many more guns and their bombardment killed huge numbers of the Jacobites, who had nowhere to shelter on the open moor.

The clans wanted to charge, but Charles did not give any orders. More and more men fell during the next twenty minutes.

Then, the clansmen on the right and centre of the Jacobite army disobeyed Prince Charles and rushed towards the enemy. This was a disaster because they ran into a trap.

Some Hanoverian Highlanders had hidden behind a wall. When the Jacobites raced past this wall, these soldiers suddenly stood up and fired into their sides. At the very same moment the soldiers in front of them fired as well. More Hanoverian soldiers came forward to help in the fighting and the charge was stopped.

The fighting did not last very long before the Jacobites were forced to turn back.

The MacDonalds on the left were preparing their attack when they noticed what was happening. They spotted Hanoverian horsemen moving forward and thought they would be surrounded and captured. Most of them fled. Some, however, continued with their attack. Many of them, including some chiefs, were killed.

Prince Charles was so shocked by his defeat that he had to be led away from the battlefield.

Punishing the Highlands

The Jacobites still had enough men to carry on the war because many of their soldiers had not reached Culloden in time for the battle. They were planning to continue the '45 when they got orders from Prince Charles: 'Let every man seek his own safety the best way he can.' He had given up. The rising was over.

Cumberland was determined that there would be no more trouble from the Jacobites. He gave orders that every man captured at Culloden should be killed. His horsemen raced around the area and killed everyone they thought was a Jacobite. However, a lot of innocent people were killed as well. After that, the Highlanders called him 'Butcher Cumberland'.

After a few days Cumberland's army marched down the Great Glen towards Lochaber. They were looking for Jacobites and killing them. They also burned their houses, especially the houses of the Jacobite chiefs.

The Royal Navy helped them. All along the west coast of Scotland sailors landed to burn houses and to ruin the crops. They also drove away the cattle because Highlanders earned their money by selling cattle. They were making sure that the clansmen would have to stay at home to look after their homeless and starving families. One Captain wrote, 'The Highlanders now curse the Prince and their chiefs for leading them to their ruin.'

Some people who were not Jacobites lost their homes and cattle because the sailors did not know who had supported Prince Charles and who had supported King George.

This picture shows the end of the Battle of Culloden. It shows the cruelty of the soldiers.

The Duke of Argyll complained that his lands were being burned. He was very annoyed because he was a good Hanoverian and his soldiers had fought for King George at Culloden.

The Government also made many new laws against the Highlanders.

These laws changed the way of life in the Highlands for ever. The attack on the clan system was one of the main causes of the Highland Clearances. Without the support of the chiefs the Gaelic language also began to decline.

So, although only some of the Highlanders had supported Prince Charles, all of the Highlands suffered as a result.

Below: 'Gillie Wet Foot' was a messenger boy in Inverness just after Culloden. He is not wearing tartan and is wearing trousers.

Highlanders had to hand over their weapons. This time the Government made sure it got all of them. Any Highlander caught with weapons was cruelly punished. When three men went to Fort William to hand over their muskets and swords they were hanged just because they had them!

Bagpipes were discouraged because they were seen as 'an instrument of war'.

Highlanders were no longer allowed to wear plaids. Instead they were made to wear trousers. The Government also banned 'tartan', the coloured designs the Highlanders had on their clothes.

The Jacobite chiefs were punished. Some were executed and the rest were made to live abroad. Their lands were taken away from them and Government officials looked after them instead.

Then the Government began its attack on the clan system. The chiefs lost much of their power over the clansmen. They were also persuaded to send their sons to schools in the south. The Government wanted them to grow up more like ordinary southern landowners than Highland chiefs.

The Hunt for Prince Charles

A 'Wanted Poster' for Prince Charles.

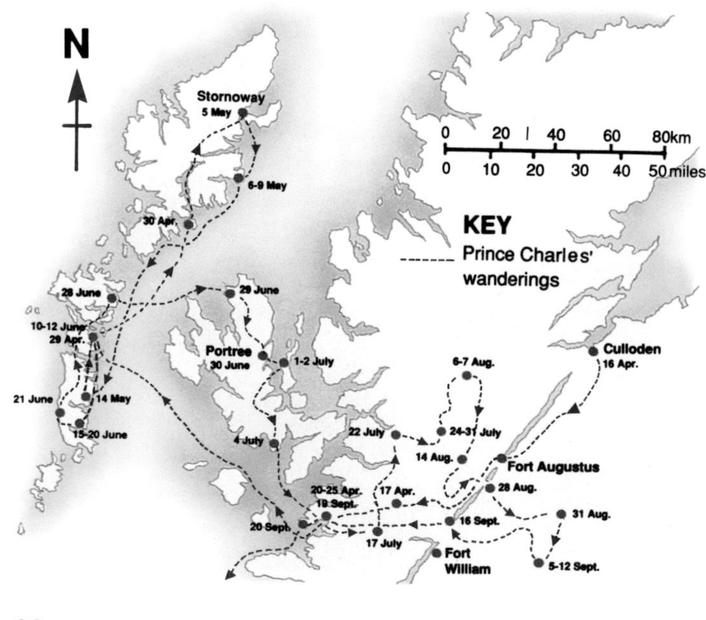

Immediately after the battle Prince Charles fled to Lochaber. He hoped to get a ship to take him back to France. However, the soldiers were after him and there was a reward of £30,000 for him. This is £3,000,000 in modern money.

No French ship arrived for the Prince. He decided to sail out to the Hebrides because he thought it would be easier to spot a French ship there.

While he was away, two French ships arrived at Loch nan Uamh. They had not heard about the Battle of Culloden and they carried weapons and gold for the Jacobites. Just as they were landing their cargo some Royal Navy warships sailed into the loch. A battle began and continued until the Royal Navy thought it had done so much damage to the French ships that they could not escape.

But during the night the French ships sailed away. They left the weapons and treasure behind and took many Jacobites to France. But they did not have Prince Charles.

He was making his way from island to island, looking out for French ships and trying to hide from the Royal Navy, which was hunting for him. Groups of sailors were searching every island and burning the homes of Jacobites as they went.

Left: Prince Charles' wanderings in the Highlands

Flora MacDonald, the real Highland lady *(left)*, and her maid, 'Betty Burke', who was really Prince Charles disguised as an Irish spinning-woman.

Prince Charles always managed to keep one step ahead of them! He was helped by local people. Some of them were not really Jacobites, but they did not want him to be captured.

His boatman, Donald MacLeod, whose sons had been killed at Culloden, said 'What about £30,000? My conscience would have got to me. Although I could have got all of England and Scotland, I would not have allowed a hair of his body to be touched.'

Many Highlanders felt the same about Prince Charles.

The Prince was almost captured on the island of South Uist. The sailors were searching the island and there were no ships to take him off it. He managed to persuade Flora MacDonald to disguise him as her maid, 'Betty Burke', and to take him over the sea to Skye. From there he returned to Lochaber, and on to Loch nan Uamh.

A French ship was waiting for him and at midnight on 19 September 1746 Prince Charles left Scotland for the last time.

'And so he left,' said John MacDonald of Borrodale, 'and left us all in a worse state than when he found us.'

But that was still not the end of the Jacobites.

After the '45

The Jacobites did not give up. They always hoped that Prince Charles would come back again.

A number of Jacobite spies came to the Highlands. Their mission was usually to collect money for the Jacobite chiefs who were living abroad. Their clansmen had to pay one rent to the Government officials in charge of their area and a second, secret, rent to their chief.

Sometimes the spies had other business. In 1752 Allan Breck Stewart went to Appin, near Lochaber. He knew that a Government official, Colin Campbell of Glenure, was going to throw some Jacobites out of their houses. But on his way to do this, Colin Campbell was murdered. Everyone thought that Allan Breck had done it, but no one could find him.

The Government was determined to punish somebody. They arrested his foster-father, James Stewart, 'James of the Glen', and put him on trial. They accused him of being 'art and part' of the murder, which means that they thought he knew all about it.

James Stewart said he knew nothing at all about the murder, but he was found guilty and hanged on a hilltop close to the place of the murder. His body was put in an iron cage and left hanging there for many years to warn local people about supporting the Jacobites.

The very next year another Jacobite spy, Doctor Archibald Cameron, brother of Lochiel, came to Lochaber. He wanted to find out what had happened to the treasure which the French ships had landed at Loch nan Uamh in 1746. Some Jacobites thought that this treasure was not being shared fairly and there were a lot of arguments.

'Doctor Archie' was betrayed. Government soldiers arrested him and took him to London, where he was hanged and then beheaded. He was the very last Jacobite to be executed.

After Culloden it was very dangerous to have pictures of Prince Charles. Jacobites kept 'secret paintings', which looked like a mess of paint. But, if they were put in the right place, the secret pictures could be seen in the reflection.

Doctor Archie - the last Jacobite to be executed.

Prince Charles as an old man in Rome.

Prince Charles got another promise of French help in 1759. Britain and France were at war again, so the French decided to help the Jacobites. The French gathered 48,000 men and 337 ships to take them across to Britain to help with a new rising.

It never happened. The Royal Navy attacked the French fleet and did so much damage that the invasion could not take place. Once again, Prince Charles was disappointed.

Indeed, the rest of his life became a disappointment. He fell out with many of the Jacobites who lived abroad and did nothing to make himself popular anywhere. He didn't even do much when his father, the Old Pretender, died in 1766, though he began to call himself King Charles III.

He lived in Rome until his death in 1788, aged 68. He had no children to take up his claim to the British throne and neither had his younger brother, Henry. After their deaths, most Jacobites accepted that King George III was their true king.

Glossary

Barracks
Buildings in which soldiers stay.

Bonnie
Scots word meaning handsome, pretty or good, e.g. Bonnie Dundee, Bonnie Prince Charlie.

Bruce, King Robert I
King of Scots 1306 - 1329. The MacDonalds believed they had helped him to stop Edward I and Edward II conquering Scotland.

Civil War (1642–1651)
The Scottish and English Parliaments fought King Charles I about his religious laws and his attempt to ignore his Parliaments and share some power with them. Charles I was defeated and killed in 1649. Charles II continued the war until he too was beaten.

Forts
Buildings for soldiers, surrounded by strong walls to protect them.

Gaelic
The language of the Gaels. It is still spoken today in the Highlands and abroad. It was badly affected when the Highlands were punished after the '45.

Highland Clearances
In the nineteenth century many Highlanders were forced to leave their clan lands because their 'chief' thought he could make more money by grazing sheep on the clan lands. Often violence was used and the Highlanders had to go and live abroad.

Lairdie
'Lairdie' is a Scots word for 'landowner', 'wee' means 'small'. The phrase 'a wee bit German lairdie' means 'a very unimportant German who is not worth bothering about'.

Lochaber
An area in the west Highlands of Scotland, which supported the Jacobites.

Lowlands
The central and southern part of Scotland. It was mainly English-speaking and was quite different from the Gaelic-speaking Highlands. Lowlanders often disliked Highlanders because they thought they were 'wild'.

MacIain
All the chiefs of Glencoe were called MacIain. 'Mac' is the Gaelic word for 'son' and this name showed that they were all descended from the very first chief of Glencoe, who was called Iain.

Military roads
Roads built by soldiers to make it easier for soldiers to travel across the country. Ordinary people could also use these roads.

Moidart
The area of Lochaber where Prince Charles first landed.

Outer Hebrides
The line of islands to the north west of the Scottish mainland.

Parliament
Members of Parliament are elected by the people to make laws and help decide how the country is governed.
The Stuart kings and their parliaments argued about how much influence parliament should have over the king's government.

Plaid
A large length of tartan cloth hung over the shoulder and secured at the waist by a leather belt.

Protestants
Christians who do not agree with the ideas of the Roman Catholic Church. They 'protested' about it and set up their own churches.

Revolution
Using force to get rid of a government.

Roman Catholics
Christians who accept the religious ideas followed and taught by the Pope in Rome.

Sheriff
Government official in charge of law and order in his area or 'shire' e.g. Argyllshire, Invernessshire.

Tullibardine, the Marquis of
He would have been the Duke of Atholl but he was a Jacobite. King George would not allow him to become Duke because he had fought in the '15 and in the '19. In 1745 he was one of the Seven Men of Moidart and he held the flag at Glenfinnan.

The Union
The Union of the Crowns in 1603, when the King of Scotland became King of England as well.
The Act of Union in 1707 joined the Scottish and English Governments and Parliaments into one.

William and Mary
Mary became Queen because she was King James' daughter. Because she was married she had to give power to her husband, so William of Orange became King William.

Further Information

Books to read

Fiction:
These books are all tales set around the time of the Jacobite risings.
The Flight of the Heron by D K Broster (Mandarin, 1993)
Gleam in the North by D K Broster (Mandarin, 1993)
The Dark Mile by D K Broster (Mandarin, 1993)
The Hill of the Red Fox by Allan Campbell Maclean (Canongate, 1984)
Quest for a Kelpie by Frances Hendry (Canongate, 1987)
Jenny by Frances Hendry (Hamish Hamilton, 1991)
An Edinburgh Reel by Iona McGregor (Canongate, 1986)
Kidnapped by Robert Louis Stevenson (Canongate, 1989)
Catriona by Robert Louis Stevenson (Canongate, 1989)

BBC Education Scotland has produced a range of resources on the Jacobites.

For TV: *The Year of the Prince* in *Around Scotland (*also made in Gaelic in *Mu Chuairt Alba).*(Transmission Spring 1995)
For radio: *A Parcel of Rogues* – a drama serial in *Scottish Resources: 10 –12.* (Transmission Spring 1995)
Software: Developed in co-operation with Strathclyde University, Jordanhill Campus – written by Fred Rendell.
Wallchart and Activities Pack: Developed in co-operation with Pictorial Charts Educational Trust; consultant: Iain Rose.

Information on ordering print support materials is available from:
BBC Education, Room 305, 5 Queen Street, Edinburgh EH2 1JF.
Telephone 031 469 4261.

Index